T0083251

ANGEL RIDING A BEAST

Writings from an Unbound Europe

GENERAL EDITOR

Andrew Wachtel

EDITORIAL BOARD

Clare Cavanagh

Michael Henry Heim

Roman Koropeckyj

Ilya Kutik

LILIANA URSU

ANGEL RIDING A BEAST

POEMS

Translated by Liliana Ursu and Bruce Weigl

NORTHWESTERN UNIVERSITY PRESS

EVANSTON, ILLINOIS

Northwestern University Press
Evanston, Illinois 60208-4210

First published 1996 in Romanian under the title *Înger Călare Pe Fiară*
by Carīea Românească. Copyright © 1996 by Liliana Ursu. English
translation copyright © 1998 by Liliana Ursu and Bruce Weigl. Pub-
lished 1998 by Northwestern University Press. All rights reserved.

Printed in the United States of America

ISBN 0-8101-1658-8 (cloth)
ISBN 0-8101-1659-6 (paper)

Library of Congress Cataloging-in-Publication Data

Ursu, Liliana, 1949–
    [Înger calăre pe fiară. English]
    Angel riding a beast : poems / translated by Liliana Ursu
and Bruce Weigl.
      p. cm.
    First published in Romanian under the title: Înger călare pe
fiară, by Carīea Românească, c1996.
      ISBN 0-8101-1658-8 (cloth).—ISBN 0-8101-1659-6
      I. Weigl, Bruce, 1949– . II. Title.
    PC840.31.R82I5413 1998
    859'.134—dc21   98-28162
                                         CIP

*For our families
and our friends*

■ □ ■ □ ■

CONTENTS

III. Memories from the Arc of the Mountains

■ □ ■ □ ■

ACKNOWLEDGMENTS

Thanks are due to editors of the following magazines in whose pages some of these poems originally appeared.

American Poetry Review: "Ruins of the Monastery at Cirtisoara," "Society of Consumers," "Prayer for Brother Alexander," "About Sacrifice," "The Mistaken Road," and "Depression before the Equinox (or Words for the Portraits of Poets Dreamed by Jan Cordua)."

Columbia Journal of Literature and the Arts: "The Key to Mystery," "Way of the Stars," and "Hierophany."

Kenyon Review: "The Russian Army at Moldova," "Mathematics," and "St. Anthony."

New Virginia Review: "Sitting on the River's Bank Not Knowing What Side You're On" and "The Intersection."

The New Yorker: "The Purification of Space for Dorothy."

Poet Lore: "February Night Eating Blackberries," "Prelude," and "Memories from the Arc in the Mountains."

Quarterly West: "Window Cut into Pine" and "My Body."

Rafters: "The Town of Pisa" and "February Night Eating Blackberries."

Salt Hill Journal: "Above Us."

TriQuarterly: "Playing with the Mirror," "What My Eyes Say," and "American Night."

The William and Mary Review: "Heart Washed Like a Brain, Europe for Sale."

The author and cotranslator wish to thank our editors at Northwestern University Press and our friends and family, including Reg, Tess, Stuart, Dan, Jean, Mihnea, Andrew, and Hanh, for their support.

Ms. Ursu also gratefully acknowledges the generosity and support of the Fullbright Senior Scholarship Program, Pennsylvania State University and its Department of Germanic and Slavic Languages and Literature, and her colleague there, Professor Michael Naydan. And thanks always to God.

■ □ ■ □ ■

INTRODUCTION

ANY HISTORY OF ROMANIAN POETRY, NO MATTER WHAT canon it attempts to establish, is bound to take note of an impressive poetic richness and diversity. For reasons having to do with the recent history of the country, which forbade direct expression, there is no doubt that poetic discourse has been a favorite medium used to explore the human predicament.

Even if one can speak of several "schools," each more or less identifiable in terms of the strategies deployed by poets in response to the proliferation of political and ideological borders that increasingly tended to isolate the individual, the poetic voices of Romania have been as distinct as anywhere else. Challenged by the same historical experience, Romanian poets have responded with a variety of intensity of resistance to borders in general, including those created by language itself. That their postmodern experiments often create a common ground as they embrace a variety of formal and stylistic breakthroughs achieved by American poets should not surprise us.

The self-renewing spirit of American poetry has made a significant impact on Romania. The brief political freedom in the late 1960s did not last long, but it lasted long enough to facilitate a variety of rich contacts, some of them with far-reaching effects. Perhaps most notable was the opening to American culture manifest in the privileged place the English language began to hold in Romanian schools, a linguistic preference that laid the groundwork for an ample reception of American literature. Not that it was only recently that twentieth-century American poets were being discovered in Romania. Ion Pillat had translated Eliot's *The Wasteland* in the early 1930s. Still, one can speak of a different, more complex response in the 1970s and 1980s. Contemporary American poetry, read in translation or in the original, deeply engaged the imagination of Romanian poets. The poet Mircea Ivanescu is most likely to come up in such a context, since no measure of his outstanding poetic achievement can be taken without considering his intimate relationship with American poetry: the forms it has assumed and the visions it mediates.

Liliana Ursu was born in Sibiu, the city that has adopted Mircea Ivanescu, but she belongs to a younger generation of Romanian poets. Her first volume of poetry was published in 1977, five years after she graduated in English from the University of Bucharest. Today her reputation is based on the publication of several additional poetry collections published over the past two decades, as well as on her noteworthy work as a translator and editor of cultural programs for Romanian Radio. There is much promise that she will become a familiar name in the English-speaking world as well. Many of her poems, including those collected here, have already appeared in important American literary journals and anthologies. Most recently, a collection of her poetry, *The Sky Behind the Forest*, translated by Adam Sorkin and Tess Gallagher, was published in England.

Reading Ursu's poems, one is provided with a clear and imaginative sense of what it means to be an Eastern European woman poet, and of the power of a mind that never ceases to seek answers to the challenges of our recent history. Lucian Blaga, one of the most important figures of Romanian modernism, also had close associations with Sibiu, which may account for Ursu's interest in his poetic vision. Not indifferent to the questions raised by Blaga and by poets elsewhere, Ursu's poetry expands our awareness of existential issues and is already becoming a locus of energy for the new Romanian poetry.

Most of Ursu's poems originate within a particular erotic or meditative mood, emerging as a landscape of feeling or as an exploratory act of inescapable givens, such as what it means to live and to love in time, an obsession most appropriate for a century that closes a millennium. An impulse toward self-irony is also therefore clearly present in these poems, as well as a powerful, almost violent engagement with words that often draws out of language an intimately revealing light against which things seem to lose their dullness and oppressiveness.

In her American poems written during 1992–93 and then in 1997 when she taught Romanian literature and culture at Pennsylvania State University as a Fulbright fellow, Ursu appears more tempted than in her previous work to sound a confessional note as she tries to make sense of her new experience and the bearing it has and will have on her personal life and her writer's life. To become an American is, above all, her chance to become better aware of her relation to the world. Ursu's response to what America discloses to her eyes and insists on being recorded becomes more ample as the American "society of consumers" brings into view its diverse characteristics, pleasant and otherwise.

Many of the poems in *Angel Riding a Beast* have their origin in seemingly nonpoetic contexts: a supermarket, a garage sale, and in images of the human element on "the margins of life." These new poems also find much of their genuine substance in the insights Ursu gains as she brings her newly Americanized vision to bear on the old questions of being, particularly her being: her roots and the Romanian sap that has not ceased to nourish her. The voice of these poems that lures the reader into sharing in this American experience and in the prospect of a wider, more worldly connection, turns its confession into an act of self-exploration that brings to light invisible bridges between the old world and the new. The idea that the farther one goes from home, the nearer one gets to oneself is reinforced in these poems by a fine cultural awareness. While profoundly marked by the inescapable and opaque reality of borders, Ursu tends to perceive such a journey as the creation of a place where things come together: where the here and the there, America and Europe, can be seen as part of the same integrating experience.

By journeying to and through America, Ursu, not so paradoxically, reaches home again and, not surprisingly, is delivered to confront and embrace the poet Ovid. One may find the Romanian connection to this Latin poet in the origins of the Romanian language and, most significantly, in the association of Ovid's banishment to the Romanian Black Sea coast. Ovid's poems of exile, *Tristia* and *Black Sea Letters,* were written in the city of Tomis at the rim of the then Roman empire, where the city of Constanta now stands. A "sandwich man, caught between two worlds," as Ursu calls him in one of her poems, Ovid was to be remembered by many poets in exile throughout the centuries; some were tempted into assuming such exile; others violently forced into it.

Ursu's fascination with Pound, himself an avid reader and student of Ovid, is also dramatized in this collection. In a sense, Ursu's crossing of the Atlantic repeats Pound's voyage in the opposite direction. Just as Pound, a passionate student of romance languages and literary traditions, put these influences to good use in his poetry, so has Ursu made significant use of her intimate contact with American poetic traditions. The reader can feel these influences in the texture of the finest poems collected here and in the freedom of the modulations of her voice, greater here than in her previous books. These influences can be traced to the immediate stimulus of this relationship.

It is Ovid, the poet of exile, with whom Ursu feels fully entitled to claim kinship. The recent history of Eastern Europe, of Romania under Ceauşescu in particular, was a strong enough incentive for many people to leave their country and accept a status that gave them little comfort. Those who stayed were increasingly deprived of a place where they could feel they belonged. Alienation as an existential condition, which informs a good deal of the present century's Western and European literature, was for Romanians a state of mind that appeared from the outside to be less complex than in other parts of Eastern Europe because it was enforced by the extremes of a mental and physical discomfort that rigidified life on all fronts. "The fire," as Ursu writes, was "turned to stone."

With their many queries about the complex notion of identity, these poems dispel the darkness of exile so that the fluidity of heart and mind becomes visible again. There is a wisely qualified affirmation of life present throughout this collection despite the pressures that threaten to silence it. Against the louder noise that speaks of the harm of history and the estrangement of love, the reader is invited to witness what Ursu calls the "purification of air." Ursu's lines "I have so many things to tell you / I've become blind and mute" represent her metamorphosis into a persona she must assume in order to reach out to her reader and evade what she calls a "domestic abyss."

Throughout this collection, there is also the powerful memory of home, not as a Black Sea of exile, but as the space in the Carpathian mountains and highlands where "the medieval walls of Sibiu" rise in an inner circle and become the starting point of the poet's journey to American and other selves. The mythical aura of Ursu's native place is a powerful presence that keeps alive for her a sense of cosmic integration. "I have never slept among such innocence," she writes, "as in the lap of that Transylvanian hill / under apple trees heavy with fruit, / the cemetery earth surrounding my hot thighs . . . " The loss of innocence that the poet experiences may threaten to render her efforts to step in time with cosmic rhythms futile, or it may bring these efforts into harmony with the challenging images of freedom and dismay now associated with America. Ursu is clearly able to confront and overcome moments of crises in her poems through the sheer act of writing them, and largely because the intimations of the eternal link between the fruit and the fall still exist for her.

To read Liliana Ursu's poems is to be made acutely aware that the "temptation to exist," in Emil Cioran's famous phrase, often demands a high cost, but it is also to be made aware of the attraction and the seduction in the ripeness of things: the soft apricot pervasive as perfume in her poetry, its shape and its juice the promise of something too precious not to deserve our effort to pursue it.

GETA DUMITRIU
BUCHAREST, 1997

I. American Night

In Bad Magic

I have the sad aura of those coming from Eastern Europe
as if from some kind of inferno.
I don't know how much of me has survived.
Our nights were stolen,
standing in line for meat, butter, or milk
or cooking all night until dawn
because when morning arrived,
as if by bad magic,
the fire had turned to stone.
During the day we walked like schizophrenics
through our world that seemed
more and more
like an asylum
because we thought one thing,
but had to speak another.
In the new world I wake,
in the middle of a night within me,
my eyes wandering across the sky,
waiting for a star
for those like me
who cannot forget.
From time to time
I get a letter from home
with the same stamp:
the crucifixion of our Lord, Jesus Christ.
For me there is no stronger star
here in the wasteland of the American sky.

The Purification of Space for Dorothy

She has hair the color of rust.
She wears a red dress
and three watches:
one for her daughter in California,
one for her daughter in New York,
and one for her sister in Scotland.
She smokes cigarette after cigarette.
She takes lithium and tells everyone
"Love, and do what you want."

She listens to the same play on the radio
and tries to convince me
that Ibsen was an American.

"He was like me, of course.
He can't be anything else."

She has a lover who works for God, she says.
"I've never met him,
so I wear this red dress
so he will recognize me
and know I am the fire."

I pretend not to understand her.

I pretend I'm in a hurry
when she asks me, almost silently,
"What do you do
up in your apartment:
do you laugh or do you cry?"
I would like to answer her.

I would like to take her hand with three watches
and caress her
as if she were an orphan,
but she is on fire.

Each morning,
below our mailboxes,
she leaves a cup full of coffee,
a pack of cigarettes
and near them, a card which says
"Live your life in beauty.
I leave these so you may partake,
as if in the body and blood of Christ."

When she meets me running up or down the stairs
she says the same thing:
"Fly if you want, but don't run.
God loves us all,
but those who fly he loves the most."

Quietly, Dorothy with rusty hair
and dress red as fire
sings
"raspberries ripen only in summer,
only when I dream of my love,"
and she shows me her empty wallet.
"Everything I touch turns to gold," she says,
"then silver, then to tears."

The Russian Army at Moldova

When a man is crucified in the year 1992 after Christ,
his last breath
produces snowstorms
on the other side of the world.

Over his children's black-and-white photograph
his heart is crucified.
How can I enter this supermarket
to buy colored Easter cards to send home
when home is nowhere now,
and my brother was crucified,
and his last home is a prayer.

Here, in this society of consumers,
I look at the crown of thorns, the nails,
the photographs of the shroud of Jesus
displayed in shop windows,
snow piling up all around,
voices from the satellites
predicting the biggest storm of the millennium.

I also take note of the high price of nails.

Longing

I'm so far from home
even the news that thieves
have broken into our country house
doesn't frighten me.
I don't even wonder about what they took,
and I avoid the verb *to steal,*
because I don't want
snow
to cover my image of that house:
my mother cooking soup,
my father
tending his tomatoes.
Already gone,
they seem so alive to me, so real,
so much
still my mother and my father,
so much the grandparents of my son.

I'm so far from home
I forget
I'm no longer in the orchard
among the apple and pear trees,
among the raspberries grown wild
from so much unshared solitude.
When I learned
that after our guests had departed,
the door had stayed open for weeks,
I laughed. I rejoiced like a child
when my son found some eggs there,
one still warm
on the desk among my books of poems.

Now, in this Texas city
without sidewalks,
the evening
losing itself to the night,
I feel the warmth of a golden chick in my palms,
pecking, with infinite tenderness,
the light around my fingers.

The Coffee Tree

I bought a potted coffee tree,
the cheapest, only ninety-nine cents,
whose label promises
it will bear tiny red fruit, hearts
pulsating in the kitchen's sad steam.
It says it must be kept in light
but not exposed directly to the sun,
what my mother would have whispered
in our garden full of blackberries:
"Don't sit in the sun,
you're too small for such light."
She could not yet know of this coffee tree
or of the roses and dandelions,
or of the heights and depths of my spirit.

I'm restless for my coffee tree
to bear its red fruit
among the poor leaves,
so I've planted in its earth
five red berries
taken from another tree,
"a natural mixture," like me,
the same combination
of strength and weakness,
the same child inside me
who will always be punished,
this tree on the sill
only a cheap metaphor
for love's red cardinal
who has deserted so many.

American Night

House of glass
from an hourglass
where a scribe washes his brush
in the blood of five apricots.
Nearby, in the house of wood,
five ordinary men
were sacrificing lambs, calves,
and blind beings newly born
to make the perfect parchment
on which the scribe would write
of the delicate princess
bowed over the white being
of the lilac in bloom.

In this American night
the moon shines over Merwin's voice
coming from the small recorder,

and my friend from the chair of anthropology
invites us to walk in the woods of Pennsylvania
to hear the owls mate.

In this American night
Lorca keeps me company
whispering
I am the elephantine shadow of my tears.

The stone I hold in my hand
is your soul, my love.

The Intersection

The neon sign howls
FOR RENT
in the middle of this American night.
The road minds its own business;
it flows and flows
house after house,
sign after sign;
the pregnant moon
bears these same obsessions.

In the bus's darkness
coming home from Philadelphia
I heard a dead man speak
for the first time:

"I'm going back to my mother
after seven years.
I don't know if she'll let me in.
I call her collect
but she won't accept the charges.
My trouble is, I married a woman
just like my mother."

Silence.
Nobody answers him.
We hear only the brakes of the bus
from time to time, a refrain.

"I was in Vietnam fifteen months.
God I wish my mother would open the door for me."

Darkness all around us.
How rare the light
for the dead man who speaks.

Way of the Stars

I live by a poor lake,
where in the morning,
gray women pick ashes
from the shore beyond fire,
beyond the loving
that they must hurry
between two Sundays.
Then the gray men come
cleaning moss and crow's silk
from the lake.

"There are no longer any fish,"
a man says,
his lip burned by his cigarette.
"We don't even have a sky above us."

The Milky Way is a road
reflected in the snow
where Mary nursed Jesus.

The Milky Way is a road of slaves
the soldiers used
to guide them
away from their wars.

Ursa Major, Great Bear,
path of stars on which Ophelia passed
in the form of a child
bearing roses
for the self she had become
in whose hands

they turn to thorns,
the flower's gold
spiraling into the sky
like cold smoke.

In New York
a woman washes dishes
and prepares to play the piano:
a piece she calls
"The Rise and Fall of Mozart."

On the path, I put my feet
into his footsteps.
In my bag, I carry bulbs
for the lighthouse
and wild berries
picked from the stars,
and a newspaper
for my love
who lives by the sea.

Hierophany

On this American hill
I am transformed:
sometimes into a loving wife,
sometimes into a witch
ready to transform this green landscape
into the blackest black,
sometimes into a synthetic cloud,
sometimes into a bare apple tree, lovers,
screaming in loneliness
under my forbidden branches.

This hill does not hold the dead in its belly,
nor does it have a tongue in its mouth.
It is simply an expensive creation
where from time to time
I come to take samples of earth.
It's like the moon's landscape
where the hill of my father's village
in Apold doesn't fit,

its tiny wooden church
pulled on wheels for three weeks,
three days and three nights
by three young men, three old men
and three boys who dragged it
over three hills, three rivers,
and across three wide roads

to bring it into the light of their home.
I have never slept among such innocence
as in the lap of that Transylvanian hill

under apple trees heavy with fruit,
the cemetery earth surrounding my hot thighs,
my dear known, and unknown dead
hung, like a chain of dandelions,
around my neck, their words
floating around me, the absolute
reality of my Transylvanian hill.

If I Lift My Eyes

Lying down this way on my back,
if I lift my eyes
I can see a country road
bordered by poplars,
which connects a village with a monastery.
I can still see the white poppies
brushing the black habit of Evlampia,
the old nun,
and I can see the river
where children swim,

and the house of the solitary man
who cultivates only
stars in his small garden
under the river.
Up there, it is summer . . .
No, it is autumn
because I can see the grape pickers
hanging from the last light
setting into this poem
which I refuse to write,

afraid that I will lose it.
Lying down this way on my back,
in this American room
if I lift my eyes
I can see the old monastery
in the vespers' light,
and the young nun, Rafaila
with the palms of an angel
which still bear the marks
of the big bell's rope.

Playing with the Mirror

I play with the mirror.
I do not set ships on fire, nor your hair,
fluttering free on another continent.
In my small mirror I try to capture
not my face, red after love,
nor the sad eyes of the icon
in my deserted house in Bucharest.

Here, in America,
my mirror reflects only a stranger.

Mirror, mirror on the wall
who's the fairest of them all?

"The Moon above Agapia monastery,"
the mirror replies . . .

One day someone will hold this same mirror
close to my mouth
to see if I'm still alive.
From my last breath
the Carpathian mountains will come,
and the sea at Sulina;
my poems of gold will come
and my poems of clay,
and my young mother
giving birth to me
into blinding July light
inside the medieval walls of Sibiu,
and I, giving birth to my own son, roses
buried under the snow.

My greedy lips will touch the mirror
as if in a last, earthly kiss,
an exercise of sadness, tragic and comic
in the innocence of the moment of my death.
I will taste apricots on my lips
which only dew from my mother's garden will cool.
I will feel on my lips
the words of my grandmother:
"Do not pick all of the fruit.
Leave some for winter's birds."

A Breugelian landscape rests quietly in my lap
like a spoiled cat,
while the mirror performs its duty,
and the TV set blares on and on
and I hear strange voices
announce from Venus:
"We have managed to make bread."

Someone in the cosmos
holds up a huge mirror
to see if we are alive.

The Sorrows of the Young Werther

What can the young man with red socks,
black shirt, shaved head
and a rat in his hand
understand about the sorrows
of the young Werther?
And if they've never met,
I'd like to introduce them,
though Goethe's Werther
would refuse to appear.
He suffered too much in his own world
to come again into ours.
In Harrisburg,
a young, pale woman
gets on the bus.
She struggles to board.
Someone rises
to help her lift the tank
of oxygen she is never without,
the translucent, slender
tubes,
like an aquatic plant,
tying her to life.
To her heart she holds an old book:
The Sorrows of the Young Werther,
proof he came to be with us, after all.

Heart Washed Like a Brain, Europe for Sale

I am the sandwich man, caught between two worlds,
one in front and one behind, pressing, testing my muscles,
my heart, my stomach, and my sex.

Below this plane, crickets sing; above, the jazz of stars,
everything waiting, like me, to be reborn.
Behind me at the gate of my house at dawn
my mother is in her long white nightgown
almost childlike, begging for one last image of me,
the wandering daughter
already on her way to America,
the car waiting, the engine warming,
my father repairing the single headlight,
poor lighthouse of the Balkans,
all of this only an illusion now.

I wish this night would break into a thousand pieces
and keep me by my family's side,
my mother still rocking herself like an orphan,
a white light radiating love.
Below me the sun, above me clouds
and the scream of clouds.
In my suitcase the words of Novica and Tutea,
their long years in prison, their years like monks,
and my prayer book, my photographs of Sibiu,
my book of poems.

"For three years, out of key with his time"
(Pound wrote of the poet)
"He strove to resuscitate the dead art
Of poetry; to maintain the 'sublime'

In the old sense. Wrong from the start—
No, hardly, but seeing he had been born
In a half savage country, out of date . . . ”

Perhaps this is the motto of my American life,
but whose motto am I,
my heart washed of all memories
and Europe for sale?
I've become the sandwich man on Broadway.
Even my mother would not recognize me,
my eyes filled with America, the stars
on and off their flag.

"An identity crisis,"
the analyst on duty would say.
Is it so? the lightning bug asks himself,
crossing the hill where I try to forget
my own Transylvanian hill, my other valley.
Valley of Happiness
is where I live now, an irony
when I think of the valley
of my Romanian home,
gold like the sky of my mother's womb
forty-three years ago, my face lined now
with as many real as imagined wrinkles,
like valleys, dug into me, like dreams,
unbearable facts, love . . .

The dice have been thrown
but I cannot see what sides are up.
Noroc! Luck! the first word I wrote on the board
for my students who come to study Romanian,
who remake the voyage of Columbus

only in reverse, sailing
toward their ancestors.
Traveling on the arc of a Latin language
they journey, without knowing,
toward my Transylvania,
my California of the old world.

In the end I will meet Ovid,
himself sometimes a sandwich man.
At the end of the millennium I will be his analyst
and he will be my shore of this sea I travel
which is called America.

September Green

Incessantly,
into the green of September,
the red leaves slip

the way my heart
rises to the lips
that dream of wild berries.

Society of Consumers

Some throw away chairs, some clothes,
some books and appliances,
all objects with short lives
laid out on the perfectly cut lawns
on the margins of life.

Today I saw a tree with red berries
thrown out,
though it still held its tiny fruit
and a Happy Birthday balloon
in its fragile branches.

In the morning, among the last stars
I see a man and a woman
in front of another house.
Because nobody wants them
they sit on the lawn.
Through their curtains
my neighbors peek,
impatient for someone
to take this man and woman away,
an apocalyptic scene
from the second millennium after Christ.

And you my love,
who mocked my lack of innocence,
who taught me the salty taste of reality,
who forced me to walk through the house
as if on a tightrope
stretched between skyscrapers,
you make me feel like the porter,

bags on his back,
dreaming of unemployment.

So as not to surrender
the innocence of my breasts
to the mirror,
and to your greedy eyes,
unbutton my blouse slowly.

II. The Key to Mystery

The Key to Mystery

Before tasting your solitude,
my body and my words are hot.
Only poor Europe
separates my door from yours.
Bow toward the window
where the woman makes lace
and without fear,
stretch your hand toward her.
The cat purring on her lap
allows herself to be stroked
like my hair
which flows
from the book you are reading.

I have so many things to tell you,
I've become blind and mute.

We sat next to each other in the theater,
watching with pity
the two armchairs on stage
in their domestic abyss.

I put on my red stockings
and became the whore in the window.
I was the wife of Rubens
in his too narrow bed in Antwerp,
but I could never deceive you.

You always found me out
and recognized my eyes and my voice
from the shore of the Black Sea

and my body
from the mountain's path.

I have so many things to tell you,
I've become blind and mute.

What My Eyes Say

My lover looks into my eyes
and calls me "my immortal one."

The doctor looks into my eyes
through his sophisticated apparatus

without the filter of love
and tells me, hidden behind the light,

"There are circles in your eyes
which point to a future of problems of the heart."

Both, I'm afraid, are right.

Mathematics

Could I put the equal sign
between my hell and your hell?
Or rather, between my heaven and your hell?
I say this in a room with only one lily,
the room where you made love's promises
and described hunting scenes
on the frozen Danube.

Again you lay your eggs in a foreign nest,
and another woman scolds you
while sewing your buttons. I long now
more than ever
for the mountain pass,
for a grass covered hill,
hidden beneath peaceful lambs.

Portrait and Renaissance Dance

I don't know why or how
the courtly dance
and the death of the artist
are connected. I imagine
he must have listened to the music.
He must have
believed
that simply by touching
the hem of her dress
in the house that rose from the lotus,
that the ocean would crash through his windows
into the room where her portrait
hung before him, their steps
a staccato of hearts,
more and more frantic in his mind.

The splendor of that dance
must have rushed into him,
but there was no trace of her,
or of her portrait,
or even of her scent;
only a small animal on the lawn,
her tail and her body
curled into the shape
of the omega
which his need for perfection
made him close,
made him circle the rope
around his neck
as he remembered those nights

his masters made him draw
the perfectly closed circle
over and over, again.

My Body

So cold, as if I had touched
a mirror in an empty room.

Our Sundays together are colder than the night.
No matter how hard my lips try,

they cannot say the words.
I recite a text from the pyramids,

and with an angel in your arms,
you throw yourself into my body

(in which you believe),
from which I departed, long ago.

Depression before the Equinox
(or Words for the Portraits of Poets
Dreamed by Jan Cordua)

The moon rises on a green path,
or is crucified on the arms of a windmill.

Discreetly, a flute accompanies
this scene from the 16th or 20th century.

In the black tunnel of the painter's telescope
a pink light appears:
portrait of Berryman as a young man
embracing the sea,
then a portrait of the poet in his iron age
on an iron bridge
from which he threw himself
into the frozen river.

In violet light, in insomnia,
Randall Jarrell bathed.
He put on his blackest coat
and entered the blackest night
until a black snow
clung to his eyes and to his soul
and he threw himself
under the wheels of a speeding car,
under the neon sign that says

                              VANITY,

the word he had carved
into the oak's bark as a child
and that had healed,

growing as the tree grew,
letting itself be swallowed
voluptuously, by the black bark.

Prelude

FOR SYLVIA PLATH

"Lift this stone from me," she whispers,
her eyes praying for light.
"Raise me from this earth
so I may see through happy eyes again,
so I may feel my lover's body
press against my breasts and my hair,
so I may feel him
swallow the lobe of my ear,
swallow my shadow,
my whole body
tattooed with his words of love and hate.

"Lift my black lace dress;
take this rouge from my cheeks.
In this grave's high grass
make me young again.
In my small purse
buried with me
you will find my lover's number.

"Call him. Tell him I am back,
that I will give him two children again,
two roses; tell him
I brought back the blackest, strongest coffee
from the grave.
Tell him I will write no more.
Tell him only that I am alive."

Window Cut into White Pine

EZRA POUND, IN MEMORIAM

A cage is still a cage,
even for the poet who looks for the sea
through bars.

From here,
in this town
torn by green and by boredom
as if washed by a Hokusai wave,
I can see Pound
as a blue spot
on a canvas
kept in a black barn
where the blind horse
slams his head against the bars of night,
more insistent than rain.

Marina Tsvetaeva

You look at me
from the ghetto of the chosen

(as you used to call us)
and I want to warm your frozen hands

to pass my hot tongue
over the marks

of a hangman's rope
burned into your moonlike neck.

I Was Picking Violets When I Heard a Howl

It's the hour when bats fly low,
touching the skin of lovers,

the hour when she paints her soul red
so he may see her from far away,

the hour when my neighbor wishes most
for his own shining path.

At night he howls to the planets,
"I am the horse of God."

The Town of Pisa

When they built the tower of Pisa
from stones of houses
destroyed by earthquake,
from flesh
stuck to those stones,

the sky shook from the weight of human bodies.

Later, the tower leaned,
eaten from the inside
by a tear.

Above Us

At one window the sun.
At the other the moon.
Within us, no one,
yet above us
the angel ascends.

Theory

Bow until you touch
flesh with the idea.

What I Hear

Someone in his despair has disturbed the great domain of the mist.
Now a green cloak is visible through that crack of light
and I hear the little chimes coming closer.

"Look, henceforth, he will bear fruit."

Ruins at the Monastery at Cirtisoara

Those walls in ruin and the dog
wandering free among the millennium
and the sheep
eating magic grass
grown from the smiles of the dead.
I had come from the mountains
and in the green stone I wore around my neck
a pack of wolves waited,
ready to jump at my lover's throat
if he betrayed me.
But what sin to think of this
jealousy
among these empty walls.

Curious children shyly touched my dress.
They had never seen such fine silk,
and I would have loved to have thrown myself
into a Greek dance for them
so that only my dreams
and my wolves of green stone would remain here,
on the ground
where I saw Isabela's scarf
wrapped around a thunderstruck tree.

Then I dreamed I was back home
in my Grandmother's
dark bedroom of lilies,
and that it rained like it rains now,
in this valley
where I'm in my tiny kitchen

drinking plum brandy,
listening to a sax
in the mist,
imagining I am alive.

III. Memories from the Arc of the Mountains

Memories from the Arc of the Mountains

The Sunday of the elections,
on the arc in the mountains,
there were watermelons
from which sleep breathed,
and a green moon

from which the sky breathed
and a glass table
on which a woman gave birth,
washed by the ocean's
waves and the scent of pines.

Ah! echo of the first thought of the newborn.
You caressed my breast with a dandelion
and like a laser it cut my life in two.
Someone removed my heart
and laid it in a barren field.

About Sacrifice

The mask that's meant to hide my face
    exposes me instead.

It is not easy
to reconcile the virgin
with the wife and the mistress.

In my house, oleander, chicory,
and many books
about deep-sea divers,
about the subconscious,
about mysticism
and the art of the fugue.

But who will protect me from myself?
Who will protect me at three in the morning
from the drunken words
that climb onto my back,
tangling my hair with violets?

Once I sailed against the current on the Danube.
On the shore
a monk picked mushrooms and wild flowers.
Another monk
ran around the same mountain
for seven years
in the sandals of the dead.

On the other shore
I saw famous and anonymous women
who had taken their own lives.

In their insomnia, and with their blood,
they wrote the magic word: sacrifice.

Sing, sirens, and you sailors,
curse this stone which is the sea.

Today, in the room facing the sea,
I discovered the dress
of the woman from the volcano,

the Christian
who had the courage
to climb to the top,
picking wild strawberries
from the rivers of lava,
throwing them into the crater's greedy mouth.

To this day her image stays
crucified against the sky.
Stars steal light from her
when the earth is cold and dark.

Computer Disk Containing One Thousand and One Variations on Silence

Christ, I made a sky from your cave.
On its walls, I inscribed your silence,
stalactites connecting heaven with hell.
In the organ's pipes
your first body lives, luminous
and aromatic like a lemon, your body
descended from the cross.
In the apricot's skin
the shade of the eucalyptus lives
under which pharaohs sleep,
the ones who died young,
dreaming bodiless of the light.

Silence lives in the tops of trees
that no body, no lips, no words
can describe.
Only she, the cross, bears this silence.

I eat silence.
You eat silence.
She eats silence.
He swallows silence.

We no longer believe
in the taste of silence.

Pilgrim

In black and white
I saw that you were still with me.
First a single blackbird descended,
then a second
pecked near my feet
buried in the snow of lambs.

Quickly I boarded the first train,
leaving this city and both of you
beyond the here and the now.
And I, your wandering daughter,
your pilgrim afraid of the snow
buried deep in my blood,
got off at Oradea
and stepped into the deep grass,
and for the first time this winter
I rejoiced.

In the park on the Cris,
a young man with frozen hands
planted small trees
into the patient earth
like you, father,
when you opened
a path for me home.

I went on until I reached the bridge
over crazy water.
If you have lied, my son had told me,
you cannot cross this bridge
or it will crumble.

I throw a coin into the water's abyss,
a candle for you, dear mother, sweet father.
Later, in the church of Mother Mary,
in the window under the cross,
I see the moon
on which a bird
has been crucified in her flight.
A child offers me daffodils
like the ones you grew, father.
They are tiny suns
lighting the night of this planet.
Small petals, translucent
fingers
of an angel riding the beast.

The Monk

This monk never knelt.
He prayed only standing.
He stretched his hands
eastward and westward,
a cross of flesh and blood.
A bird sat on his outstretched arm
one rainy morning.
The warm light from his body
made her stay,
where she built her nest.

He could not return to the monastery.
He could not leave her without shelter.
Rain and dew quenched his thirst.
In the middle of the forest
he became a living cross
on whose arms the chicks were born,
learned to fly,
and in the dark remoteness,
exercised their freedom.

Standing upright, unmoving,
but weaker and weaker,
and more deeply buried in the light,
the monk lost all track of time.
Touched by the small wings
he shivered with joy.

What cross of light
comes toward us?

Cismigiu Park

Do not speak so loudly.
I have a cosmic hearing.
I can hear even the dead of Siberia,
and those from the prisons of Aiud.

Last day of the year in Cismigiu.
I can see my poet friends
swimming perfectly
under the heavy ice of the river here,
under the ice of all cities and all towns.
I can hear the voice of a friend whisper
Love your God
because you won't find a greener path than His
under your feet.
She lives as she says in her poetry,
"away from this world
like mystery," praying,
her knees torn by stones and grass,
by too much silence.

Everyone wants something from her:
a piece of her heart, her silky body.
How sweet the skin of a poet.
How fragrant her heart.
A wave carries her
away to the pyramids.
A howl fills her lungs. Rails
run through her words
like the unbroken silver thread
through mirrors.

In this frozen park in the Balkans,
near a small lake,
I dream in full winter
of the tiny star
above Bethlehem.

The Small Truths

So simple to utter the small truths:
I love you, mother.
I understand you, my son.
I pray for you all.
I pray.

When the small flower
sends her small truth
into the world
I don't think of the fallen dove
covered with newspaper,
or the fists that knocked my hair
down
as if into a tomb,
or the hatred like a radioactive cloud
invading my memory.

When these truths disappear,
I lift my eyes to the cross
from which forgiveness comes.

I was moving through the dust of years
when on the Sunday of the Blind
I looked for my soul and couldn't see it.
I began to pray, my God,
and You covered my body with mud.
You gave me back my eyes.

Through a Town Lost in the Balkans

My walk through this lost Balkan town
is a map of hazard,
but I am talking now about spring,
the hungry season
ready to tear at its cubs,
the monotonous days of March,
the town
filling with the desert dust
buried deep in peoples' hearts.
I pass by a bank
and hear talk of the rate of the dollar
in Tokyo and in New York.
I pass a common house
and see the old teacher, starving to death,
coming out to the street
to beg for some bread.
With the little money I have
I buy stinging nettles, bread
and a book by Baudrillard
about fatal strategies.
At home I boil the nettles
(they have iron and will kill
any winter left in you).
I ache for my mountains,
for the purity of wood,
for the immensity of the word "sky."
Little by little,
these aches
through which I learn my way,
descend into the drift of this town
lost in the Balkans.

February at the Sea

The light of seashells
enters what's left of my day
in Bucharest.
I left behind only some strange eyes.
Not yours, my love, not yours.
I get up. I fall. I get up again.

In the hallway
on the tenth floor of this hotel
called "The Pearl,"
some women wait for me:
journalists, opera stars, an actress.
I read poems with angels and beasts, and later
we talk of love,
but mostly of violence.
The sun begins to set.

I go down to the beach.
I descend into dream
as if into a red sea;
as if into a black sea.
Some patches of snow
in this February desert
try to befriend my solitude.
Free, I breathe the last light
of the day and of the sea.
The waves bring a path of burning
crocuses to my feet.
I walk into the blessed water
to feel the touch of a garden
beneath my winter feet.

The Beginning of March

The daffodil is wrapped in many shawls
like this moment is wrapped
in many layers of memory.
The crocuses hardly dare open a leaf
to try its dark ring of color
against the still biting cold,
against the bull-like hide of the earth.
So much delicacy, oh God, where does it go?

The cat stares at the world outside the window,
singing birds rousing her lust.
Only I pretend not to see the lilac buds
that scratch at my window with their green.
Only I, deaf and dumb to the world around me,
continue to speak of everything
patiently, and with love,
forgetting my body
in the room of mirrors
that was my childhood.

Prayer for Brother Alexander

Today, everyone talks of courage,
but what the hell do they know,

those who never entered a monastery,
who never fought in a war,

about the message of Brother Alexander,
Officer of the Red Army

who would not obey the order
to burn the church

but instead
left a poorly written message:

Pray, for Brother Alexander.
In this starless rain

I think more and more often
of the bees, and the nun's dying hives

under blossoming apple trees,
and the black flowers after the fire.

Temptation of the Abyss
(or Letter from the City of Vikings)

Above and below me the stage;
surrounding me,
the lake and its stone shadow, the castle,
and inside me
the prompter, prompting my life.

Inside me
an excellent nightclub
grows full of empty glasses and bottles.
I align my feet at the edge of the diving platform,
at the limit of darkness and light,
always at the limit.

On stage Arlettle and Claude tell the same story
"full of sound and fury and signifying nothing."
Mimes of my soul,
they show me the way through the labyrinth
with their voices, their bodies, and their despair.

My red stockings of anxiety
devour younger and younger boys.
Anxiety takes us by our hands
outside the lost city of the Vikings, directly
into the snow-covered fields.

Rehearsing for Spring

I have never written about a bear,
though often I write of violets.
Today, at the beginning of spring,
I open my father's diary:

"April 3. I watered the strawberries. I planted tomatoes.
I fixed the fence and I dug three holes for cherry trees.
In the afternoon, I took the nun who broke her arm trim-
ming trees to the monastery. When I returned from town
I wrote a letter to my daughter in America.

"April 5. I cut the roses. I fixed the roof. I worry about the
apple trees. A wave of cold has come, and they are in blos-
som. I put some drops in the blind eyes of my neighbor,
Radu. His house is so clean. He asked me to look at his
icons, to check that he'd dusted them all. He'd hung them
upside down, the saints staring strangely at the ceiling. I
set them right and did not tell him how I'd found them.
The earth in my garden is well rested. I could plant more
strawberries. They are big and juicy. They are called Poc-
ahontas. Liliana sent them from America with her letter
and a poem for me. Maybe tonight dear old God will give
us rain. Far away, above Bucharest, I see lightning."

A blackbird sings at my window. Boringly it rains.
In this room Lucky feeds her kittens
who have just begun to see, their small, shiny eyes
like beads spread out in the desert of the day.
I am reading Maxine's poems about horses and small beings.

66

I see the small nun
in the garden of the Monastery,
nursing the beehives.
Honey and wax, wax and honey.
I feel like saying these words endlessly.

Another nun makes candles in the last light.
The painter covers Christ's wounds
with a thin stratum of the wax of candles
lit for the dead and the living.
I remember the honey
poured over thick, black bread
in my grandmother's kitchen. In the sky
my mother is still painting the Easter eggs.
In this poem
I try to save them all.

February Night Eating Blackberries

When the mountain becomes only a small flame,
when the sea retreats on an old dusty postcard . . .

A pagan god climbed up my spine tonight
to reach the stars
from where he brought me blackberries.
You, in the supermarket in San Luis Obispo,
buy a magazine that offers new facts about witches.
You put on your antisentiment flak vest,
your vest of Aztec coins,
and your sunglasses. You chew tobacco
and wait to be reborn,
bored with so much death.

It is quiet in the house that still smells of blackberries
and my spine is almost healed.
But how can I put violets in my hair
when there is so much winter there,
when the she-wolf gives birth each night
in the sky above me, killing all blackberries.

My little boy asks for clothes for his evening prayer:
Before God you must not be naked, he says.
He kneels before the icon,
then crosses his teddy bear,
his book of fairy tales
and his pillow, and I forget
outside it is still February.

Sitting on the River's Bank
Not Knowing Which Side You're On

To fall, to get up
and walk toward yourself
as if toward a new death.
Long ago you died your old death
when your lover slapped your face
the first time.
The second, the third deaths
don't matter any more.

Blow into my palms to warm them.
The hot air from your lips
raises all the dead from my memory.
But better not to talk about my skin
tattooed by the needles of sadness,
poisoned with your talk of love.
Instead, let us talk of the apricot's fine skin,
the subtle hymen
you won't be punished for breaking.
Or let us talk about the skin of the oak
after rain,
as if we had another hundred years
on this earth, but please,
don't make me talk about exile.
About exile we must howl.

Among the branches of this hundred-year-old oak,
I read the words of another exiled friend.
When I long for our country
I go to the platform built for tourists
along the Berlin wall

to remind myself of the other side.
I look into the night's eyes
but see only automatic weapons
and uniformed robots
deflowering the light,
and after all of this,
you still ask: What is longing?

St. Anthony

From the stars the hand of a child throws cherries at us.
From the lake the hand of a child throws strawberries at us.
From the church bells the hand of a child throws dew at us.
The body of the book becomes young again and speaks.

From the mountain of olives, an echo.
From the ship of the seven sleepers, a whisper.
What a waste of eyes, thoughts, arms, in this world.

Have pity on us
you with a clay body like ours, rotting in the ground.
You among the dead with your living tongue.

You who keep tenderness alive in your arms,
your tongue turned into the word,
preaching the lessons of light to the fish.
Star of Spain, the diamond of poverty called to you.

You who hold pity in your arms
and leave one ray of your aura
over our bowed heads.

At the Top of the Mountain

At the top of the mountain,
between the loggers' poor café
and the kiosk of newspapers and books,
four human beings wait
for the bus to town:
a philosopher, a shepherd's wife,
and a couple on their honeymoon.

First one hears the chains of the bus tires
grind like the oars of a slave ship,
then steam rises from the hot engine
which has just climbed
high through the snow,
only to go down again,
a Sisyphus of wheels and steel.
"Terrifying as any angel," Rilke whispers

with the lips of the young bride
who boards the bus first.
The shepherd's wife, her cheeks flushed,
quickly crosses herself,
frightened by such terrible words
and then calmly places on the seat beside her
her newly baked bread

big as the wheel of a cart
and some fresh cheese
shaped like a star
and packed in a nest of spruce limbs by her husband.
So much light rises from this food

that the philosopher, blinded,
takes the seat behind her.

And the groom
listens to his headphones
and then falls asleep
to the rocking of the bus.
Quietly,
on his shoulder grown from the night,
his young bride cries.

The Mistaken Road

How strange when we come back from the shore,
we always lose our way home,
or maybe this is normal
on such a day when left is right
and right is left
and all signs point toward us.
We entered a village
in the mountains of Dobrogea
among torn nets, goats,
and a beached, abandoned ark
that seemed to support the mountain.
You wanted to photograph the ship
but I did not allow it.
I was afraid an ocean
would open under us and swallow everything.

Another time
you almost struck a hen on the road,
and when you stopped
we found the ground was made of fish
and we had been traveling
on a silver island,
and looking more closely,
I understood
that we were little fish ourselves,
and that each bone in our bodies
ached because a man and woman
drove over us,
trying to tell us something
from their red car,
and in his faded shirt,
at the police station, George,

fisherman of the Danube
whom we saved from drowning,
had stolen a floating light
from the big river
to take to his roof,
a buoy for troubled ships.

"Oh God," he says, "how I love to sit
late at night
when I come back from the water
and watch the light and the stars
flickering on my roof."

And what remains of all this?
A pair of oars
hanging in the attic.
A photograph of us
standing among huge nets
spread on the shore
and the wild goose
you shot down
that April morning
who in the stiffness
of a stuffed bird
scolds us from the wall.

She scolds us for keeping
the canary in her cage,
and scolds you
for throwing the black blanket
over me
to make me believe
it is night
and I should sleep.

■ ☐ ■ ☐ ■

WRITINGS FROM AN UNBOUND EUROPE

Words Are Something Else
DAVID ALBAHARI

Skinswaps
ANDREJ BLATNIK

*My Family's Role in the World Revolution
and Other Prose*
BORA ĆOSIĆ

Peltse and Pentameron
VOLODYMYR DIBROVA

The Victory
HENRYK GRYNBERG

The Tango Player
CHRISTOPH HEIN

A Bohemian Youth
JOSEF HIRSAL

Mocking Desire
DRAGO JANCAR

Balkan Blues: Writing Out of Yugoslavia
JOANNA LABON, ED.

Compulsory Happiness
NORMAN MANEA

Zenobia
GELLU NAUM

Rudolf
MARIAN PANKOWSKI

*The Houses of Belgrade
The Time of Miracles*
BORISLAV PEKIĆ

Merry-Making in Old Russia and Other Stories
The Soul of a Patriot
EVGENY POPOV

Estonian Short Stories
KAJAR PRUUL AND DARLENE REDDAWAY, EDS.

Death and the Dervish
MEŠA SELIMOVIĆ

Fording the Stream of Consciousness
In the Jaws of Life and Other Stories
DUBRAVKA UGREŠIĆ

Angel Riding a Beast
LILIANA URSU

Ballad of Descent
MARTIN VOPĚNKA

The Silk, the Shears and *Marina*
IRENA VRKLJAN